597

What Is the Proof for the Resurrection?

Ralph O. Muncaster

HARVEST HOUSE PUBLISHERS
Eugene, Oregon 97402

Cover by Terry Dugan Design, Minneapolis, Minnesota

By Ralph O. Muncaster

Are There Hidden Codes in the Bible?

Can You Trust the Bible?

Creation vs. Evolution

Creation vs. Evolution Video

How Do We Know Jesus Is God?

Is the Bible Really a Message from God?

What Is the Proof for the Resurrection?

WHAT IS THE PROOF FOR THE RESURRECTION?
Copyright © 2000 by Ralph O. Muncaster
Published by Harvest House Publishers
Eugene, Oregon 97402

Library of Congress Cataloging-in-Publication Data

Muncaster, Ralph O.
    What is the Proof for the Resurrection? / Ralph O. Muncaster.
        p. cm. — (Examine the evidence series)
    ISBN 0-7369-0324-0
        1. Jesus Christ—Resurrection—Biblical teaching. I. Title.

BT481 .M82 2000
232.9'7—dc21   99-053610

Printed in the United States of America.

00 01 02 03 04 05 06 07 08 09 / BP / 10 9 8 7 6 5 4 3 2 1

Contents

Biblical References

Matthew 26–28—Jesus described as King

Mark 14–16—Jesus described as Servant

Luke 22–24—Jesus described as Savior

John 13–21—Jesus described as Son of God

Why Investigate Easter?

What if there is a God?
What if there is a divine plan for mankind?
What if a person's soul or spirit exists for eternity?
What if there is a heaven and hell?
What if the biblical ultimatum of heaven
and hell is true?
What if committing to Jesus is the
only answer for heaven?

If these things are true, then *understanding and accepting God's plan is the single most important thing to discover in life.* More important than the next vacation. More important than the next golf game. Even more important than the next paycheck. And our choice regarding that plan will affect us forever. It's a choice that can bring real joy here on earth. A choice that can mean "no more pain and no more tears" forever. Or a choice that will lead to eternal horror.

Would God expect us to accept His plan on faith? Yes and no, because history can never be "proven." Instead, *evidence* is the only basis for verifying historical fact. Does evidence exist for the Easter resurrection? Absolutely. *There is far more evidence for the resurrection than for any other single event in the history of the world.*

Often people don't embrace a relationship with God because they fail to investigate and understand their beliefs. Some people are taught wrong beliefs from birth, which they never objectively challenge. Some people are misled by individuals who cleverly tamper with facts and tell people what they want to hear. And some people just don't care. Yet abundant evidence exists for the first Easter and the tremendous message it brings to mankind. Hence, we might reject God out of apathy . . . or out of pride . . . or for many other reasons. But we have no basis to reject God for lack of evidence if we take time to seek it. As the Bible says, "Men are without excuse" (Romans 1:20).

First Easter—The Real Issues

The *real issue* of the first Easter—Jesus Christ—
has been analyzed *far* more than anyone
in the history of the world.

Did Jesus Really Exist?

1.

*The existence of Jesus
is one of the best-
established facts in history.*

Thousands of early
manuscripts that survived
major eradication attempts
provide greater support
than is available for any
other accepted historical
fact. And the confirmation
of early Christian martyrs
who were alive at the time
of Jesus is undeniable
(pp. 12–23).

What Is Easter All About?

2.

*The essence of Easter
is man's relationship
with God.*

Man is separated from God by sin. God requires a perfect sacrifice to redeem man's relationship with Him. It was provided, for those who accept it, with the death of His only Son. The resurrection (Easter) verifies Jesus' role and ultimate victory over sin.

The Old Testament is filled with hundreds of messages preparing man for Jesus and verifying His arrival (pp. 24–35).

Why Does Jesus Matter?

3.

*Joy on earth
and forever.*

Strength to face
any challenge.

Eternal life with God.

Everyone must make a choice to accept or reject the One who lovingly gave His life for us. No decision is also a choice . . . of rejection. Jesus offers the above free gifts to anyone (pp. 46–47).

The First Easter—Key Historical Facts

1.
The Empty Tomb
The tomb was empty.
No corpse of Jesus was ever found. Early enemies would have certainly done anything to find the body and silence the resurrection story forever. The tomb was heavily guarded to prevent theft (pp. 18-21).

2.
Scripture Prophecies
Detailed prophecies foretold many facts about the Messiah (pp. 24–33):
Who He would be,
What He would do,
When He would come,
Where He would be born.

12.
Archaeology
Archaeologists believe they have located the site of Jesus' birth. Other compelling evidence of the existence of Jesus and extensive knowledge of the resurrection have been discovered (p. 22–23).

11.
The Jewish Record
Even those people violently opposed to Jesus provide historical evidence, including hundreds of prophecies, prophetic feasts, and references in writings such as the Talmud (pp. 16–17, 29–33).

9.
The Disciples' Martyrdom
Eleven people who *certainly knew the truth* of Jesus and the resurrection, willingly—even joyfully—died to support the historical account. It reflected a purposeful effort of disciples to ensure the historical record remained intact, in spite of the cost of eventual execution (p. 20).

10.
Historical Martyrs
Millions of people, many able to communicate with eyewitnesses, willingly died to preserve the historical record (p. 20–21).

3.
Jesus' Own Prophecies
Jesus Himself prophesied precise details of His death and resurrection. This substantiates His divinity (pp. 34–35).

4.
Paul's Change
A prominent leader of the persecution of Christians gave up wealth, position, and status once he encountered the risen Jesus. Paul recorded most of the New Testament (p. 21).

5.
The Other Witnesses
Many people witnessed the risen Christ . . . over 500 people saw Jesus after the resurrection (1 Corinthians 15:6). If the resurrection had been false, the Gospel accounts being circulated would never have stood the test of time (pp. 16–21).

6.
The Manuscript Explosion
Never before or since has such an explosion of reporting of an event ever occurred, as with the birth, life, and resurrection of Jesus. The historical record was available to many eyewitnesses (pp. 12–15).

7.
Rapid Church Formation
Events caused the formation of the church—a body that survived the most focused and intensive persecution of all time (pp. 18–21).

8.
Non-Christian Evidence
Several non-Christian writers recorded facts about Jesus, His disciples, and the resurrection (p. 16–17).

The Historical Setting

The stage was set perfectly for the first Easter.

The World Situation

Political stability—Never before or since has such a large percentage of the world lived at peace under a single government. The Roman Empire had expanded to include much of Europe, Africa, and Asia. About half of the world's 138 million people were governed by Rome. And the peace known as *Pax Romana*, admired throughout history, lasted 200 years.

In 44 B.C. Julius Caesar was assassinated, and his throne went to his great-grandnephew Octavian, who was given the title Caesar Augustus. After defeating Mark Antony and Cleopatra, Augustus ruled from 27 B.C. to A.D. 14. Augustus began the great peace reforms and ordered the worldwide census which caused Joseph and Mary to travel to Bethlehem at the time of Jesus' birth (Luke 2:1).

Transportation—For the first time in history, an elaborate network of highways and sea routes made transportation throughout the empire relatively easy. This was vital to the rapid spread of Christianity.

Communication—The world was becoming unified as the level of education increased, and the language of Koine Greek was becoming common (the dialect of the New Testament). As a result, it was easier and quicker to spread new ideas and thinking across a multicultural world than ever before.

Bethlehem, Nazareth, and Jerusalem

Jerusalem was the most prominent city in the Middle East. Along with being the political and religious center for the Jewish people, it was a regional seat of government for Rome and the residence of Herod.

Nazareth was on a major trade route from the ports of Tyre and Sidon, both known for vice and prostitution (as was Nazareth). The great city of Sepphoris, just four miles from Nazareth, was the capital of Galilee in Jesus' youth and was being rapidly expanded to honor its new leader, Herod Antipas. As carpenters, Joseph and Jesus almost certainly spent time there. (Excavation of Sepphoris is far from complete.)

Bethlehem of Judea was a small rural town, located a few miles south of Jerusalem. Even in Jesus' day, Bethlehem had significance as the burial place of Rachel (Jacob's wife), the place of courtship of Ruth and Boaz, and the birthplace of King David.

Friday or Thursday Crucifixion?

Some people want to "force" the crucifixion to a Friday due to references of a Sabbath the evening after Jesus' death (normally starting Friday evening). Friday is an option, but John 19:31 clarifies that the forthcoming Sabbath was the "*special* Sabbath," which always occurs the day after Passover. So a Thursday crucifixion would have as much validity as Friday.

A key issue of debate is Jesus' own prophecy that "like Jonah" He would be (dead) for "three days and three nights" (Matthew 12:40). A Thursday crucifixion seems to meet this prophecy better. However, idioms used at the time could also permit a Friday crucifixion, assuming the reference was to the days of Friday, Saturday, and Sunday.

Did Jesus Exist?

Virtually all major religions—even those opposing Him—acknowledge the existence of Jesus. For hundreds of years, Jesus' existence was as widely accepted as Abraham Lincoln's existence is today. Only in relatively recent history have some people challenged it. Possibly in a few thousand years, Mr. Lincoln's existence may be challenged as well.

Christian Historical Records[4]

The magnitude of the Christian record stands far above any record of anyone who has ever lived upon this planet. Existing early manuscripts exceed 24,000. The earliest were written within 25 years of His death. No work of antiquity approaches the Bible's documentary credibility, including *all* works we accept as historical fact. Some examples are:

Major Existing Manuscripts	Early Records	Event Until First Existing Manuscript
Julius Caesar—*Gallic Wars*	10	1000 years
Pliny the Younger—*History*	7	750 years
Thucydides—*History*	8	1300 years
Herodotus—*History*	8	1300 years
Homer—*Iliad* (Second most prevalent writing)	643	500 years
The New Testament	24,000+	25 years

The vastness of the number of accounts of the resurrection is particularly extraordinary considering that:

1. *Jesus was not in a position of public importance.* He was not a

king, not a religious leader, nor a general. Relative to Rome, Jesus came from a small, distant town and was a lowly carpenter with a scant three-year ministry. *Rome hardly knew of Him* until testimony of eyewitnesses later threatened political/religious stability.

2. *The records survived the most intensive eradication effort* of all time. Rapidly growing in number, Christian witnesses were killed, written records were burned, and anyone professing belief in Christianity was executed. In A.D. 303 an edict was issued to destroy all of the world's Bibles. People found with Bibles were killed.

3. *There was no printing press, and the world population was low.* The number of surviving early manuscripts is absolutely staggering considering they were all *hand copied* by a far smaller population base. Only 138 million people existed at the time, with no automatic duplication methods for the printed word. What motivated such extensive work?

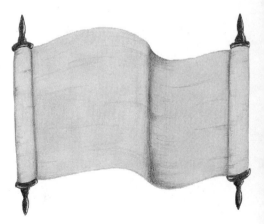

Was the incredible *quantity* and *survival* of the Christian record a miracle, or just senseless expansion of a myth? Why haven't other religions with more prominent leaders, with lifelong ministries, and with less persecution produced similar evidence? Something *major* happened.

Manuscript Documentation

The position of Jewish scribe was one of the most demanding and esteemed jobs in biblical times. After training for years, scribes were allowed to practice the profession only after age 30. Often referred to as doctors of the Law, they joined the priests in the teaching of the Law.

Scriptural Copy Rules[4]

Recording of Holy Scripture was a serious responsibility. So important was exact reproduction that Old Testament scribes were forced to adhere to demanding rules anytime a manuscript was copied:

1. Scrolls—special paper, ink, and surface preparation required.

2. Tight specifications—specified column number, 37 letters per column.

3. Master used—no duplicates of duplicates.

4. Each letter visually confirmed—no writing of phrases.

5. Distance between letters checked with thread.

6. Alphabet—each letter counted and compared to original.

7. Letters per page counted and compared to master.

8. Middle letter of scroll verified to be the same as the master.

9. One mistake—scroll was destroyed (i.e., master scrolls).

Proof of Authenticity

Not surprisingly, critics of the Bible, especially those knowledgeable of the prophecy miracles, suggest that the Bible was changed, altered, and somehow mishandled. Commonly, people claim the Bible was in the control of the Roman Catholic Church, which supposedly had "opportunity and motive" to change Scripture to meet its purpose. Such critics miss some key facts. There are two indisputable sets of records that mankind has in its possession today that were *not* historically controlled by the Christian church and verify the authenticity of the message contained in the words of the Bible we read today:

The Septuagint

Almost 300 years before Christ, the world was becoming so accustomed to Greek that the language of Hebrew was becoming "lost." It was deemed more important to translate the Bible into a common language than to try to teach everyone Hebrew. A group of 70 elite scholars was assembled to translate the Scriptures into Greek. The result was a document called the Septuagint (meaning "seventy"), compiled around 250 B.C. (Several copies were made by the techniques of the scribes above.) Today, we still have copies of the early translations. The Septuagint message is consistent with the Bible.

The Dead Sea Scrolls

Any doubt regarding the accurate transmission of manuscripts was erased in 1947 with the discovery of hundreds of scrolls buried in caves for nearly 2000 years. Many were written before 100 B.C. Comparison of biblical books with recent Jewish copies shows virtually no change in words or even letters.

Non-Christian Evidence

Very few written works *of anything* in history exist from the period of A.D. 30 to 60. All works from A.D. 50–60 are said to fit in bookends only a foot apart.[4] Nero's killing of Christians in A.D. 64 led to non-Christian writing about Jesus.

Thallus (circa A.D. 52)—Historical work referenced by Julius Africanus. Explains the darkness at the time of Christ's death as a solar eclipse. While an eclipse did not occur in that period (pointed out by Julius Africanus), reference to Jesus' death was stated as a matter of fact.

Josephus (circa A.D. 64–93)—This Jewish historian referenced Jesus, His miracles, His crucifixion, and His disciples. Also referenced are James, "brother of Jesus who was called the Christ," and John the Baptist.

Cornelius Tacitus (A.D. 64–116)—Writing to dispel rumors that Nero caused the great fire of Rome in A.D. 64, he refers to Christians as the followers of "Christus," who "had undergone the death penalty in the reign of Tiberius, by sentence of the procurator Pontius Pilatus." The resurrection was called "the pernicious superstition."

Writings from Jewish Rabbis

Several passages from the Talmud and other Jewish writings clearly refer to Jesus Christ.

- "Hanging" (on a cross) of Jesus on the eve of Passover [written: circa A.D. 40–180].

- Identifying Jesus and the names of 5 disciples.

- Healing in the name of Jesus.

- Scoffing at the "claim" of a virgin birth, and implying "illegitimacy."

Pliny the Younger (circa A.D. 112)—As governor of Bithynia (Asia Minor), he requested guidance from Rome regarding the proper test to give Christians before executing them. (If they renounced the faith, cursed Jesus, and worshiped the statue of Emperor Trajan, they were set free.)

Hadrian (circa A.D. 117–138)—In response to questions regarding the punishment of Christians who drew people away from pagan gods which affected the sale of idols, Hadrian said that they be "examined" regarding their faith (similar to the response to Pliny the Younger).

Suetonius (circa A.D. 120)—A historian who wrote about events in the late 40s–60s A.D. that identify Christ, the "mischievous and novel superstition" of the resurrection, and the fact of Christians being put to death by Nero.

Phlegon (circa A.D. 140)—Referenced by Julius Africanus and Origen—referred to "eclipse," earthquake, and Jesus' prophecies.

Lucian of Samosata (circa A.D. 170)—Greek satirist Lucian wrote about Christians, Christ, the crucifixion, Christian martyrs, and "novel beliefs."

Mara Bar-Serapion (circa A.D. 70+)—A Syrian philosopher wrote from prison to his son comparing Jesus to Socrates and Plato.

Did the Resurrection Occur?

As prior pages indicate, the crucifixion of Jesus was especially well documented and accepted as fact. The crucial question then becomes, Did Jesus rise from the dead, proving His claim to be God incarnate? Or did something else happen with His body? Or was He never dead at all?

A key to this issue is the extreme *local importance* placed on handling this execution. Jesus' powerful, insightful speaking and many miracles had led the populace to request that He become king. This began to threaten the local political stability of the Romans and the religious power of the Jewish leaders whom Jesus openly criticized. Both the absolute death of Jesus and the protection against a hoax were critical, since Jesus had claimed He would overcome death. Furthermore, He had already raised other people from the dead. As a result, all precautions were taken to secure His corpse (Matthew 27:62–66).

The Bible implies the cause of Jesus' death was cardiac arrest, indicated by blood and water from a spear thrust (medical experts confirm this). To secure the body, a Roman guard was placed outside the tomb. Such a guard would have consisted of 16 soldiers, with a disciplined rotation for sleeping at night (every four hours, four would switch). The guards all faced the rigid Roman penalty of crucifixion if they slept outside of the assigned shift or deserted their post. The idea that all guards were asleep, considering the death penalty, is especially unreasonable. To further ensure safekeeping, a two-ton stone[4] was rolled in front of the tomb with Pontius Pilate's seal on it. Breaking the seal without the official Roman guard's approval meant crucifixion upside down. The central issue—unexplainable by Jewish leaders, especially in light of the many precautions—is . . .

What happened to Jesus' corpse if He did not rise from the dead as indicated in the Gospel accounts?

The official explanation is that the disciples stole the body while the guards were asleep (with the priests protecting the guards from the governor). This story was necessary only because *no one could produce a dead body of Jesus*, which would have stopped the resurrection story forever. Is a theft of Jesus' body even remotely possible given that:

1. *All 16 guards would have had to risk the penalty of crucifixion* by sleeping while on duty or deserting. Surely at least one guard would be awake.

2. *The disciples were in a state of shock, fear, and disarray,* having seen their Master crucified. Is it reasonable to think they quickly created a brilliant plan and flawlessly executed it on the Sabbath day of rest?

3. *What possible motive could the disciples have?* If Jesus was not the Son of God as He claimed, stealing the body would create a lie with no apparent benefit, and death *for no purpose* for the disciples.

Analysis of Other Explanations

- *Was Jesus really dead?* Crucifixion was more routine and was a longer, more visibly excruciating death than the electric chair is today. Is it likely that such professional executioners would not know death? The final spear thrust to the heart area was to ensure death. For such a political threat, they would be certain. If Jesus was not dead, what are the chances that a barely living person could move a two-ton rock from the inside of a tomb and escape a full Roman guard unnoticed?

- *Was the body stolen at night?* Recognizing that no flashlights nor infrared sensors were available then, is it likely that a band of scared disciples carrying torches could bypass a full Roman guard, move a two-ton rock, and not be noticed? Furthermore, the Sabbath greatly limited movement. And again, for what motive?

Eyewitnesses to the Truth Died to Tell the Story

Martyrdom for a belief is not unique. But what kind of person would die for a *known* lie? Someone insane? Would *all* the disciples face hardship and death for a known lie? The disciples were with Jesus constantly for three years. They would certainly know the truth of the resurrection. Lying would serve no purpose since Jesus' ministry would then be moot. Yet historical records and reports about the disciples indicated they all died cruel deaths for their beliefs (except John). James was *stoned*, Peter was *crucified* upside down, Paul was *beheaded*, Thaddaeus was killed with *arrows*, Matthew and James (Zebedee) faced *sword deaths*, and other believers were *crucified*.

The Testimony of the Catacombs

Underneath Rome lie some 900 miles of carved caves where over seven million Christians, executed for their beliefs, were buried. Other believers hid and worshiped in these caves during the height of Christian persecution. The earliest known inscriptions in the walls were dated A.D. 70. Some early occupants probably communicated directly with eyewitnesses of Jesus. Since about A.D. 400, the Catacombs were buried and "forgotten" for over 1000 years. In 1578 they were rediscovered by accident. Today they can be seen as silent memorials to many who died rather than curse Jesus or bow down to an emperor's statue. Christian martyrs differed greatly from other world martyrs in that *historical facts were the foundation of their beliefs—facts verifiable at the time—not just ideas.*

Hostile Witnesses Turn Christian

Paul, a leading executor of Christians, gave up wealth, power, and comfort upon seeing the resurrected Christ, then wrote most of the New Testament. Two Sanhedrin members (not present when the Sanhedrin sentenced Jesus to death) were secret disciples. Unbelieving natural brothers of Jesus later became believers *after the resurrection.*

Archaeological Evidence

Archaeologists have discovered substantial support about many details of Jesus' life. Some examples include:

Indirect Resurrection Evidence [2]

Evidence that the people in Jesus' time believed in the resurrection is found on caskets of bones (ossuaries) discovered in a sealed tomb outside Jerusalem in 1945. Coins minted in about A.D. 50 were found inside the caskets, dating the burial within about 20 years of Jesus' crucifixion. Markings are clearly legible, including several statements reflecting knowledge of Jesus' ability to overcome death. Examples of writings (in Greek) of hope for deceased loved ones include: "Jesus, Help" and "Jesus, Let Him Arise." The caskets also contain several crosses, clearly marked in charcoal. This is powerful evidence that early Christians believed in Jesus' ability to triumph over death. It also ties the idea of victory over death to the cross.

Prior to the resurrection, "grave robbing" was not considered a serious offense. The resurrection changed that. An inscription found on a tomb in Nazareth warns that anyone found stealing from the tombs would receive the death penalty. Scholars believe the inscription was written as early as Tiberius (circa 37 B.C.) or as late as Claudius (A.D. 41–54). In the latter case, it would have been shortly after the crucifixion. Naturally, Jesus' hometown of Nazareth would be an obvious city of "interest" to officials.

Jesus' Burial Shroud?

A burial shroud (Shroud of Turin) is believed by many people to be the actual burial shroud of Jesus (Matthew 27:59; Mark 15:46; Luke 23:53).

Items supporting its authenticity are:

1. Tests that confirm fiber type and small particles of limestone dust unique to the region

2. Confirmation of blood, in wounds precisely as indicated in the accounts of Jesus' unique execution

3. Confirmation of a crucifixion as a likely cause of the type of image created . . . matching a deceased body

4. Coins on eyes dated about the time of Jesus' crucifixion

Some experts have been able to mimic creation of the shroud's image using today's technology. Some believe it to be a complex fourteenth-century hoax. The ultimate issue of its use for Jesus, however, will never be certain.

Jesus' Birthplace[5]

To us, a "stable" is a type of wooden barn outside a home. In Jesus' day, stables were often within courtyards of homes or in caves outside. The actual site believed to be the "stable" of Jesus' birth was identified relatively shortly after His resurrection. Early authors (Jerome and Paulinus of Nola) indicate it was "marked" about the time of Hadrian (circa A.D. 20). Archaeologists have never seriously disputed it. The site is a cave located beneath the Church of the Nativity in Bethlehem.

The Prophecies—Statistical "Proof"

Although history can never be "proven," enormous statistical probability is often viewed as proof by scientists and mathematicians. From a statistical viewpoint, God's involvement in the life of Jesus is "certain."

As indicated earlier, the prophecies contained in the Old Testament were written long before Jesus. The Dead Sea Scrolls provide irrefutable evidence that these prophecies were not tampered with over the centuries. Of the 469 prophecies contained in the Old Testament that would have been fulfilled, 467 have been verified (we have no record of fulfillment of two). Perhaps the most fascinating prophecies are those about Jesus.

Who	Jesus' Ancestors in Prophecy:
David	2 Samuel 7:12–16; Jeremiah 23:5
Jesse	Isaiah 11
Judah	Isaiah 11
Jacob	Genesis 35:10–12; Numbers 24:17
Isaac	Genesis 17:16; 21:12
Abraham	Genesis 12:3; 22:18
Shem	Genesis 9:26,27; 10
What	
Virgin birth	Isaiah 7:14
Birth of eternal Savior	Isaiah 9:6,7

Savior to Jews and Gentiles	Isaiah 49:6
Miracle worker	Isaiah 29:18; 35:5,6
Rejection by Jews	Isaiah 53:1–3, Psalm 118:22 Matthew 21:42–46

When

Prophecy of the Date of Palm Sunday	Daniel 9:20–27—Although complex until understood, this prophecy made about 535 B.C. predicted Jesus' final entry into Jerusalem *to the day*. The prophecy states:

Daniel's "Seventy Sevens"

- 69 periods of 7 (years) will pass from the decree to rebuild Jerusalem until the coming of the "Anointed One" (*Messiah*, in Hebrew). This dates Jesus' entry into Jerusalem on Palm Sunday.

- After that time the Anointed One will be cut off (Hebrew: *yikaret*, meaning a sudden, violent end—crucifixion).

- And after that time the city and the temple will be destroyed.

Prophecy: Daniel, a Hebrew, received the prophetic revelation in 535 B.C. Using the *Hebrew* definition of a year (360 days) we find:

69 times 7 years = 173,880 days

The decree to rebuild Jerusalem was given by Artaxerxes on March 14, 445 B.C. (first day of Nisan that year—Nehemiah 2:1–6).

Using the *actual* 365-day calendar, along with adjustments for leap years and the final scientific adjustment (leap year is dropped every 128 years), we find this number of days brings us precisely to[7]:

April 6, A.D. 32

History: Jesus' ministry began in the *fifteenth year* of Tiberius Caesar (Luke 3:1), whose reign began in A.D. 14. A chronological analysis of Jesus' ministry shows three years leading up to the final week, in A.D. 32.

The Royal Observatory in Greenwich, England, *confirms the Sunday before Passover that year to be . . .*

April 6, A.D. 32

Other prophecy elements were fulfilled as well:
- Jesus was crucified three and a half days later.

- The Romans destroyed the city and temple in A.D. 70.

Where

Precise City of Jesus' Birth	The Bible (Micah 5:2) specified that Jesus would be born in Bethlehem, in Ephrathah (i.e., Judea—there was another Bethlehem closer to Joseph's home in Nazareth).

Other Prophecies

- King on a donkey (Zechariah 9:9)

- Suffering, rejected (Isaiah 53:1–3)

- Crucified, pierced (Psalm 22:16)

- Cast lots for clothing (Psalm 22:18)

- No bones broken (Psalm 22:17)

- Given gall and wine (Psalm 69:20–22)

- Pierced with a spear (Zechariah 12:10)

- Posterity to serve Him (Psalm 22:30)

- Betrayal by friend (Psalm 41:9)

- Betrayed for 30 pieces of silver (Zechariah 11:12)

- Silver cast on temple floor was used to buy potter's field (Zechariah 11:13)

Amazing Prophecy

Statistics experts estimate the probability of all these prophecies coming true in *any* one man is about one chance in 10^{99}—less than the odds of correctly selecting one electron out of all the matter in the universe, or essentially zero *without divine intervention*.[4]

When Was the First Easter?

Historical scholars agree that *any date* of *any event* in ancient history is subject to uncertainty. There is more information about the date of the death of Jesus than of any other date in ancient history. However, because the date is also tied to other historical events which have uncertain dates some variation of opinion exists. A few scholars have identified alternative dates that also appear to meet historical and biblical facts within the boundaries of historical uncertainty.[3] Research indicates the most likely date of the first Easter is:

Sunday, April 13, A.D. 32

The facts defining the date of the resurrection are fairly straightforward. Jesus' ministry started in the fifteenth year of Tiberius Caesar (Luke 3:1), whose reign historically is assumed to have begun in A.D. 14. Jesus' ministry lasted a little more than three years, leading up to the final Passover. Therefore, the year would be A.D. 32 (A.D. 14 + 15 years + 3 years). The Royal Observatory at Greenwich, England, indicates the actual date of the day of Passover that year was Thursday, April 10, A.D. 32. Hence, Jesus was crucified the morning of April 10 and placed in a grave *before sunset that evening* when the special Sabbath—the first day of the Feast of Unleavened Bread—began. (By Jewish reckoning, *the start of any day is at sunset the evening before[7]*).

The First Easter Week, April, A.D. 32

4 Friday	5 Saturday
Jesus— Bethany with Lazarus	Sabbath

6 Sunday	7 Monday	8 Tuesday	9 Wednesday	10 Thursday	11 Friday	12 Saturday
Palm Sunday triumphal entry	Cleanses temple	Pharisees confronted	Last Supper sunset— Passover	Crucifixion Passover	Special Sabbath Feast of Unleavened Bread	Sabbath

13 Sunday	Note: While scholars may dispute precise dating of ancient events, the overwhelming evidence
Resurrection	validating these events and the sequence has not been in question.

Of significance is the role of Jesus as the Passover Lamb. The historic timing of Jesus' death, as shown above, makes Him literally fulfill the role of the "Passover lamb" at precisely the right day and the right hour.

Feasts of Israel Foretell Jesus

God commanded seven specific feasts to be celebrated centuries before Christ (Leviticus 23). The first three feasts perfectly parallel the redemption role of Jesus. The fourth, Pentecost, relates to the church age, and the final three feasts relate to the second coming of Christ. Like many prophecies in the Bible, the feasts had both a historical meaning and a prophetic significance. Ironically, today millions of Jews annually celebrate the feasts that are symbolically tied to the Christ that many Jews reject.

Timing of Feasts

God commanded Moses to make Nisan the first month of the year (Exodus 12:2). Three key "new beginnings" took place during the same festival period in Nisan:

The Jewish Calendar (Months)	
1. Nisan	7. Tishri
2. Iyyar	8. Marcheshvan
3. Sivan	9. Kislev
4. Tammuz	10. Tebeth
5. Ab	11. Shebat
6. Elul	12. Adar

1. *Noah's ark* came to rest— 17 Nisan (Genesis 8:4)

2. *Israel* freed as a nation— 14 Nisan (Exodus 12:51)

3. *Jesus* crucified and resurrected—14, 17 Nisan

Spring Feasts

Passover .... 14 Nisan

Unleavened Bread .... 15–21 Nisan

Firstfruits ..... day after Sabbath

Pentecost .... 50 days after Firstfruits

Fall Feasts

Trumpets .... 1 Tishri

Atonement .... 10 Tishri

Tabernacles .... 15 Tishri

29

Passover (Exodus 12)

First established to remind the Hebrews of God's deliverance from the bondage in Egypt (the exodus described by Moses), Passover has many direct ties to Jesus:

Passover—Deliverance from Physical Death

• Passover: 14 Nisan •

• Lamb selected: 10 Nisan (Exodus 12:3) •

• Lamb to be perfect, without blemish (Exodus 12:5)

• Blood of lamb saves those using it •

• Lamb to have no bones broken (Exodus 12:46) •

Passover Supper

• Observed by Jewish family (Exodus 12:3) •

• "To remember" gift of God's salvation (Egypt) •

• Broken, unleavened bread—signifies humility and • God's "gift" to His people, regardless of status

• Bitter herbs—"bitterness" of bondage in Egypt •

• Third cup of wine, the "redemption" cup, represented • the blood of the lamb—God's blessing

• Wine mixed with warm water—signified • "blood of sacrificial lamb"

• Sacrificial lamb to be last food eaten—all of • lamb to be consumed, remainder burned

Did You Know?
John the Baptist was the first to recognize Jesus as the "sacrificial lamb" the day after he baptized Jesus (John 1:29).

Crucifixion—Deliverance from Spiritual Death

• Crucifixion: 14 Nisan •

• Christ selected: 10 Nisan (Palm Sunday) •

• Christ perfect, without sin (1 Peter 1:19) •

• Blood of Christ saves those accepting it •

• Christ had no bones broken (John 19:36) •

Lord's Supper

• Observed by "family" of Christ •

• "To remember" God's gift of salvation (eternal) •

• Broken, unleavened bread—signifies humble, sinless •
Christ—God's sacrificial Gift to all who accept Him

• Bitter herbs—"bitterness" of bondage to sin •

• Third cup of wine, the "redemption" cup, represented •
the blood of Christ—God's blessing

• Blood of Christ mixed with water (John 19:34) •
—"final evidence" of sacrifice of Christ

• Christ broke bread after the lamb—new ordinance •
showing He superseded the traditional sacrifice

Feast of Unleavened Bread

This feast, tied directly to the Passover, begins the following day—on the fifteenth of Nisan. It starts as a "high holy day" (a special Sabbath) and continues for seven days. Many Jews simply regard it as part of the Passover celebration. Yeast, a symbol of sin, is forbidden during this feast—presumably to remind the Hebrews of the moral purity that was to follow the deliverance from Egypt.

Now that we understand the full significance of Christ's crucifixion, we can have a greater understanding of the ultimate symbolism of the feast. Those accepting the sacrifice of Christ (represented by the Passover) can immediately receive freedom from the bondage of sin with the forgiveness offered by God.

Feast of Firstfruits

The original feast was designated by God to be on the "day after the [Saturday] Sabbath" following the Passover (Leviticus 23:9–11). This was the exact timing of the day of the resurrection (the "first Easter"). Traditionally, the feast was to celebrate the new harvest—the firstfruits from "new life" born in the spring. It acknowledges God's blessing by offering gifts back to God.

Now we can recognize the ultimate meaning of the Firstfruits celebration in anticipation of the resurrection. Several aspects are significant:

> *First*—the priests waved a sheaf of grain to the Lord (Leviticus 23:10), not a single stalk. It represented the entire harvest—all belonging to God. With one sacrifice *many* can be saved through Christ . . . *all* will be dealt with.

Second—the offering had to be accepted by the Father (Leviticus 23:11). Jesus also acknowledged He had to first "ascend" to the Father to be received before being appropriated by the people (John 20:16,17).

Third—The feast of Firstfruits celebrates *new life*. Likewise, acceptance of Christ's sacrifice and triumph over death means *new life*.

Feast of Weeks—Pentecost

This feast was exactly 50 days after Firstfruits (Leviticus 23:15). Exactly 50 days after the resurrection the "church age" was ushered in to both Jews and Gentiles with the outpouring of the Holy Spirit (Acts 2). Prophetic implications include:

- *Two loaves of bread*—This sacrifice represented the two component parts of the church, Jews and Gentiles, being reconciled before God (Leviticus 23:17).

- *Leavened Bread*—This was a seemingly odd command considering that saying leaven was representative of sin and was excluded in all other feasts. It suggests that although freed from the bondage of sin through Christ, we are never sinless.

Other Feasts

Trumpets—prophetic of the second coming of Christ (and regathering of Israel).

Atonement—prophetic of national atonement for Israel upon repenting and receiving Jesus.

Tabernacles—prophetic of earthly reign of Christ.

Jesus' Own Prophecies

The many prophecies made by Jesus Himself
are important because:

1. Perfect accuracy verifies the prophecy was "from God"
   (Deuteronomy 18:19–22).

2. Since He claimed to be the Messiah and the Son of God, it
   verifies the claims of Jesus Christ.

Prophecy from Jesus includes several immediately verified by
people around Him [e.g., Jesus told a centurion his servant would
be healed—Matthew 8:5–13].
Other prophecies refer to
judgment, to heaven, or to the
end of the world. Jesus told His
disciples that His precise
prophecy of His death and
resurrection was so that when it
happened they would believe He
was the Messiah (John 13:19).
The Jews realized that only God
knows the future.

What Does the Word *Easter* Mean?

It disturbs some people that the name for the important holiday of Christ's resurrection, *Easter*, may have been derived from the name of the pagan goddess of the spring. Other Easter customs—bunnies, eggs, baskets—follow pagan traditions. Scholars believe it is more likely that Easter was derived from an Old German root for *rising sun* or *east*.[1]

Virtually all Christian (or occult) holidays involve name and custom crossovers. Such crossovers need not detract from a holiday's personal significance. More important issues are the meaning and heart behind the celebration.

The Resurrection Prophecies of Jesus

1. That He would be *betrayed* (Matthew 26:21; Mark 14:17–21; Luke 22:21,22)

2. *Who* would betray Him

3. *When* He would be betrayed

4. That His *disciples would desert Him*

5. That *Peter would disown Him* three times (Matthew 26:33,34; Mark 14:29,30; Luke 22:31–34)

6. That He would be *crucified* (John 3:14–16; 12:32–34)

7. That He would *die and then be resurrected*:

   • First prediction   (Matthew 16:21–28; Mark 8:31–9:1; Luke 9:21–27)

   • Second prediction   (Matthew 20:17–19; Mark 10:32–34; Luke 18:31–34)

   • Third prediction   (Matthew 26:2–5; Mark 14:1–9)

8. That on the *third day* He would rise from the dead

9. That He would return from death to *meet the disciples in Galilee* (Matthew 26:32)

Was the Resurrection Physical?

Some people (and even organizations) have tried to minimize or even disclaim Christ's physical resurrection. Why? Perhaps because it undermines Jesus' claims to deity. A prophet had to be 100 percent accurate to be a prophet of God, and clearly Jesus indicated that He would rise again physically from the dead (John 2:19–22). Or perhaps people want to diminish the role and power of Jesus. The facts clearly state that the resurrection was both real and physical.

The resurrection was a *highly* significant event to Jews in the area. The Saducees and Pharisees debated fiercely over the concept of resurrection long before Jesus. After the first Easter, people argued over it, people imprisoned others for it, people even died for it. In the days immediately following the Resurrection there was no doubt that *many* people believed that Jesus appeared again in a physical form.

The accounts recorded in the New Testament stood the test of eyewitness examination. They could have easily been challenged

Did Jesus Walk Through Walls?

Sometimes people read the Bible and conclude Jesus must have been able to pass through walls (John 20:19). Perhaps he did.

First, it should be pointed out that the Bible does not specifically state that Jesus went through walls. He appeared in a closed room, which may have included His knocking, then entering the room.

However, it is quite conceivable, perhaps even probable, that Jesus actually did pass through walls. Quantum physics now suggests that there are several dimensions beyond the four we know. Understanding these dimensions[6, 8] helps us understand how a supernatural God (Jesus) may have "walked through walls."

by contemporaries. In the earliest days, there is no record of anyone claiming Jesus was an apparition (ghost) or a mass hallucination or any other sort of "mere spirit being." For the resurrection to have any meaningful significance, it had to be a resurrection of the body, as Christ Himself indicated. Several references support this.

Eating, Drinking, Touching

Can a spirit eat? Drink? Touch? There is no historical evidence of any spirit-form taking on human functions unless it became human first (e.g., angels becoming human).

Jesus, on the other hand, specifically made a point of verifying His physical existence by eating and drinking *after* the resurrection (Luke 24:37–43).

Can a spirit or hallucination be touched or felt? Thomas, the most doubting of the disciples, certainly believed that touching was a primary criterion for "proof." Jesus specifically appeared to Thomas (and the others), challenging him to see the nail prints in His hands and *touch* His side (John 20:25–28).

Jesus—Was He God?

Christians claim that Jesus was (in reality) God appearing to the world in human flesh. The Christian concept of the one God of the universe includes three distinctly different, yet inextricable parts: the Father, the Son (Jesus), and the Holy Spirit. Though somewhat difficult to understand, analogies have been made to H_2O which can exist as water, ice, and gas . . . or to light, having quantum, wave, and physical properties.

Did Jesus Think He Was God?

Many times Jesus referred to His own deity, both directly and indirectly. Although Jesus confirmed that He was the Messiah (Mark 14:62,63), He did not use the term *Messiah* to refer to Himself, perhaps to differentiate His deity from the widespread expectation of a *human* Messiah. Jesus used the terms "Son of Man" and "Son of God" often. Both referred to His divine nature (Daniel 7:13;14; Matthew 26:63,64). Jesus also used the specific words *I am* (*Ego eimi* in Greek, *Ani bu* in Hebrew) on several occasions (e.g., John 8:56–58). God used these same words to describe Himself to Moses. Jesus also states specifically that He and God are "one" (John 10:30).

And Jesus clearly indicated He had authority over issues controlled only by God, such as forgiveness of sin (Mark 2:5–10), the timeless power of His words (Matthew 24:35), and reception of glory (John 17:5). Perhaps as significant was Jesus' acceptance of worship (Luke 5:8; John 20:28). The intense monotheistic foundation of the Jews would absolutely forbid any worship of anything but the one true God. Overall analysis of Jesus' life—His compassionate miracles, His perfect lifestyle, and His love—indicate that His claims alone are trustworthy, and perhaps the strongest evidence of His divinity.

Did Other People Consider Jesus to Be God?

The disciples clearly came to view Jesus as God in human flesh, and they worshiped Him as such (Luke 5:8; John 20:28). Certainly, the witnessing of the resurrection and the transfiguration (Matthew 17:1–5) provided irrefutable evidence to them. New Testament writers and early Christian writing define Jesus to be God . . . *our Lord* . . . here on earth (1 Corinthians 8:6, 1 Timothy 2:5).

Is There Other Evidence of Deity?

Many people say that Jesus' miracles are evidence of deity. But miracles have been recorded as being performed by other individuals (in the Bible and elsewhere). The Bible states that perfect fulfillment of prophecy proves God's intervention (Deuteronomy 18:21,22). The odds of all Old Testament prophecies about Jesus coming true in *any* one man is beyond statistical possibility without divine intervention (pp. 24–27). And Jesus prophesied with perfect accuracy regarding such things as the precise timing of His death, the detailed manner of His death, His resurrection, and His later appearance in Galilee. Prophetic perfection combined with a claim to be God verifies Jesus' deity.

Why Do People Reject Jesus?

The evidence regarding Jesus is so overwhelming that it seems incredible that many people still reject Him. After all, the promises of inner peace and joy on earth and eternal life in heaven are not bad promises . . . and they're easy and free. Rejection of the Messiah, however, should not be surprising. It was often prophesied (Isaiah 53:1–3; Psalm 118:22; Matthew 21:42–46; Luke 16:19–31).

Ignorance—Perhaps the greatest reason for nonbelief in Jesus is ignorance. Most people take far too little time to investigate their religious beliefs. As a result, world opinion often becomes the basis for the most important issue in life. Views about Jesus may come from a family belief, friends, or a dominant church in the community. People sometimes think a church is teaching biblical Christianity when it's not. We are individually responsible for comparing teaching to the Bible. In the end, it doesn't matter what the reason is, if you are wrong. Nor does sincerity matter. As history has shown too often, people can be very sincere, yet sincerely wrong.

Apathy—Many times people have a false sense of security that God will take care of everyone. This idea is sometimes accompanied with the thought that hell doesn't exist, or that God will send everyone who "tries to be good" to heaven anyway. The Bible reveals that God's promises are reserved for *His people*, and there are many reasons why others "don't hear" (Matthew 13:11–43). The reality and horror of hell is clearly stated, including the narrow path to get to heaven, which is available to all (Matthew 7:13).

Fear—Some people fear that becoming a Christian means "giving up fun" or living a strange, secluded life without friends.

Nowhere in the Bible does it say that we must start a dull life and turn away from having parties with other people. It says the opposite. The Bible promises that knowing Jesus will let us live life to the fullest (John 10:10). And not only will such freedom draw us to have fun with friends, the Bible says even the angels in heaven throw a party when we accept Jesus as Lord (Luke 15:10).

Tradition—This reason for rejecting Jesus is often the strongest. But we are each accountable for our own actions. Even society doesn't send parents to jail for their children's crimes. Jesus knew He would, at times, cause people to break away from traditional family beliefs (Matthew 10:21,22).

The Influence of Evil

Fully understanding why people reject Jesus requires recognizing the existence of supernatural agents of evil, who are every bit as real as God and agents of good. The Bible extensively acknowledges demons, Satan, and deceitful evil influence. The goal of evil is to do whatever it takes to draw people away from Jesus. One step off the path is all it takes—such as a different "kind" of Jesus, or a stubborn resistance to asking Him to direct our life. And the world is filled with such evil trying to draw us away. But sincerely asking God to reveal the truth will overcome evil (pp. 46–47).

Answers to Common Questions

How do we know the Bible is accurate?

First, the integrity of original biblical manuscripts has been demonstrated by the vast number of *manuscripts*, precisely copied during the time of eyewitnesses and verified as unchanged by the Dead Sea Scrolls (pp. 14–15). Secondly, *archaeology* has shown complete consistency with what we know as the history of the world. Third, hundreds of ancient *prophecies* contained in the Bible and showing 100 percent accuracy indicate divine guidance and accuracy (pp. 24–27). And finally, the Bible is 100 percent consistent with established facts of *science* . . . corroborated by many of the finest scientists in the world today.

Why do some people claim the Bible has contradictions?

After hundreds of years of challenge, the accuracy of the Bible has stood the test of time. Common types of misunderstandings include:

1. *Details that once seemed to contradict science or archaeology.* Often our information is too limited to know that the Bible is right. For many years scholars believed the earth was flat, while the Bible indicated a spherical shape. Likewise, critics scoffed at the mention of the early Hittites, or cities like Sodom and Gomorrah—all thought to be nonexistent, yet verified as fact today. Scientists have recently "proven" Einstein's definition of the universe (consistent with the Bible), which has superseded Newton's more limited view.[6] The list goes on and on. As archaeology and science learn more, the Bible is verified and has yet to be proven wrong.

2. *Different accounts by different authors.* Details contained in different Gospels may at first seem contradictory. However, the accounts simply report events from different vantage points. For example, Matthew records that Mary Magdalene and "the other Mary" went to the tomb. Mark records Mary Magdalene and Mary, mother of James, and Salome as going to the tomb. Luke records "the women," and John records Mary Magdalene. Are the reports contradictory? No. Different people reported different facts. Placed side by side, they just give a more complete picture of what happened.

The Chronological Visit *to the Tomb* [9]

The three woman went to the tomb, saw a "young man" who told them of the resurrection and also told them to go tell the disciples. They left and returned with Peter and John, who viewed the tomb. The disciples then "returned home" and the women stayed. At that time, Jesus appeared to Mary Magdalene.

Like witnesses to an event today, when all testimony is pieced together, it makes perfect sense and a more complete picture is given.

Are Heaven and Hell Real?

The Bible extensively reviews heaven, hell, Satan, angels, and demons in many of its 66 books. Surveys show that many more people believe in heaven than in hell. Some nonbiblical religions even deny that hell exists. Yet, Jesus actually spoke more about hell than about heaven. So it would *not* be wise to ignore hell. Jesus' parable in Luke 16:19–31 gives us a very poignant warning regarding heaven and hell.

What the Bible Says About Heaven and Hell

Heaven	Hell
Wonderful (2 Corinthians 12:1–4)	**Eternal torment** (Mark 9:43–49)
Worth giving up all (Matthew 13:44–46)	**Separation from God** (Luke 16:19–31)
A place where God dwells (Deuteronomy 26:15)	**A place where Satan dwells** (Revelation 20:10)
Perfect—no pain (Revelation 21:1–4)	**Full of sorrow** (2 Peter 2:4–9)

It would *seem* wonderful if there was only a path to heaven with no hell. Not surprisingly, false prophets attempting to design religion for man's desires try to do away with hell, or convince man that he is God. The Bible is specific concerning the path to heaven, and indicates that other paths lead to hell.

How Do We Know What Religion is Right?

No religion is "right" in and of itself. The Bible is about man's relationship with God—the right way and the wrong way. Any religion that is totally consistent with the Bible's teaching is right. Any with teaching that is counter to the Bible is wrong.

So the reliability of the Bible as a guideline is vital. As indicated, the original biblical manuscripts are a miracle in and of themselves. Evidence of reliability includes: (1) an explosion of credible, corroborative writing, (2) verifiable *at the time* by eyewitnesses, (3) with eyewitnesses dying for testimony they could affirm to be true, and (4) with many other people, able to know historical facts, also dying for the same beliefs. If the New Testament is true, then the Old Testament is also broadly verified by Jesus (Luke 16:16,17) by over 700 cross-references, by the Dead Sea Scrolls evidence, and by "mathematical proof" of hundreds of prophecies.

A problem arises when man starts changing or adding to the Bible. Several things would indicate that such inspiration is not from God. First, the Bible commands us not to add to, delete, or change it (Revelation 22:18,19). Secondly, Jesus verified it would not change (Luke 16:17). And third, why would a perfect God change His original, perfect Word? The Bible is very clear that the path to heaven is defined as Christ:

| John 14:6–9 | Matthew 27:51–53 | John 3:16 | Ephesians 2:8 |
| Acts 4:12 | Colossians 1:15–23 | John 6:48–58 | Hebrews 10:26–31 |

Avoiding False Gods—The Bible warns against the following false gods:

- A god that is *not* a *single* God of the universe (having *no* peers—including man) is *not* the God of the Bible (1 Timothy 2:5; Isaiah 44:6).

- A god *not* manifest as God the Father, God the Son, and God the Holy Spirit is *not* the God of the Bible (Luke 12:8–10; John 1:1,2,14; Acts 5:3,4).

- A god that does *not* proclaim Jesus Christ as the ultimate sacrifice for redemption of those committing themselves to Him, is *not* the God of the Bible (Mathhew 27:51–53; Mark 14:24; John 6:48–58; Acts 4:12; Colossians 1:15–23).

How Can We Ensure the Right Relationship to Go to Heaven?

When Jesus said not all who use His name will enter heaven (Matthew 7:21–23), He was referring to people who think using Christ's name along with rituals and rules is the key to heaven. A *relationship* with God is *not* based on rituals or rules. It's based on grace, forgiveness, and the right relationship.

How to Have a Personal Relationship with God

1. B*elieve that God exists* and that He came to earth in the human form of Jesus Christ (John 3:16; Romans 10:9).

2. A*ccept God's free forgiveness* of sins through the death and resurrection of Jesus Christ (Ephesians 2:8–10; 1:7,8).

3. S*witch to God's plan for life* (1 Peter 1:21–23; Ephesians 2:1–5).

4. E*xpress desire for Christ to be Director of your life* (Matthew 7:21–27; 1 John 4:15).

Prayer for Eternal Life with God

"Dear God, I believe You sent Your Son, Jesus, to die for my sins so I can be forgiven. I'm sorry for my sins, and I want to live the rest of my life the way You want me to. Please put Your Spirit in my life to direct me. Amen."

Then What?

People who sincerely take the preceding steps automatically become members of God's family of believers. A new world of freedom and strength is then available through prayer and obedience to God's will. New believers also can build their relationship with God by taking the following steps:

- Find a Bible-based church that you like, and attend regularly.

- Try to set aside some time each day to pray and read the Bible.

- Locate other Christians to spend time with on a regular basis.

God's Promises to Believers

For Today

But seek first his kingdom and his righteousness,
and all these things [e.g., things to satisfy
all your needs] will be given to you as well
(Matthew 6:33).

For Eternity

Whoever believes in the Son has eternal life,
but whoever rejects the Son will not see
life, for God's wrath remains on him
(John 3:36).

**Once we develop an eternal perspective, even the
greatest problems on earth fade in significance.**

Notes

1. Elwell, Walter, A. *Evangelical Dictionary of Theology*. Grand Rapids, MI: Baker Books, 1984.
2. Green, Michael. *Who Is This Jesus?* Nashville: Thomas Nelson, 1992.
3. Hoehner, Harold W. *Chronological Aspects of the Life of Christ*. Grand Rapids, MI: Zondervan, 1975.
4. McDowell, Josh and Wilson, Bill. *A Ready Defense*. San Bernardino, CA: Here's Life Publishers, Inc., 1990.
5. McRay, John. *Archaeology and the New Testament*. Grand Rapids, MI: Baker Book House, 1991.
6. Muncaster, Ralph O. *The Bible—Scientific Insights*. Mission Viejo, CA: Strong Basis to Believe, 1996.
7. Rosen, Moishe. *Y'shua*. Chicago: Moody Bible Institute, 1982.
8. Ross, Hugh, Ph.D. *Beyond the Cosmos*. Colorado Springs, CO: Navpress, 1996.
9. Smith, F. LaGard. *The Daily Bible in Chronological Order*. Eugene, OR: Harvest House, 1984.

Bibliography

Encyclopedia Britannica. Chicago: 1993.

Free, Joseph P. and Vos, Howard F. *Archaeology and Bible History*. Grand Rapids, MI: Zondervan, 1969.

Freeman, James. M. *Manners and Customs of the Bible*. Plainfield, NJ: Logos International, 1972.

Hanegraaff, Hank and Geisler, Norman. *The Battle for the Resurrection*, audiotape. San Juan Capistrano, CA: Christian Research Institute.

Josephus, Flavius. *The Complete Works of Josephus*. Wm. Whiston, trans. Grand Rapids, MI: Kregel, 1981.

Keely, Robin. *Jesus 2000*. Batavia, IL: Lion Publishing plc, 1989.

McBirnie, William Stuart, Ph.D. *The Search for the Twelve Apostles*. Wheaton, IL: Tyndale House Publishers, 1973.

McDowell, Josh and Wilson, Bill. *He Walked Among Us*. Nashville: Thomas Nelson, Inc., 1993.

Missler, Chuck. *The Feasts of Israel*, audiotape. Coeur d'Alene, ID: Koinonia House Inc., 1994.

Reader's Digest. *ABC's of the Bible*. Pleasantville, NY: 1991.

Reader's Digest. *Who's Who in the Bible*. Pleasantville, NY: 1994.

Rosen, Cecil and Moishe. *Christ in the Passover*. Chicago: Moody Press, 1978.

Ross, Hugh, Ph.D. *The Fingerprint of God*. Orange, CA: Promise Publishing Co., 1989.

Shanks, Hershel, ed. *Understanding the Dead Sea Scrolls*. New York: Vintage Books, 1993.

Shepherd, Coulson. *Jewish Holy Days*. Neptune, NJ: Louizeaux Brothers, 1961.

Strauss, Lehman. *God's Prophetic Calendar*. Neptune, NJ: Louizeaux Brothers, 1987.

Walvoord, John F. *The Prophecy Knowledge Handbook*. Wheaton, IL: Victor Books, 1984.